EAL
13140005411797

201[illegible] and Past Papers with Answers

the library IN EAST AYR

National 5 BUSINESS MANAGEMENT

SQA National 5 BUSINESS MANAGEMENT

2015, 2016 & 2017 Exams
and 2017 Specimen Question Paper

Hodder Gibson Study Skills Advice – National 5 Business Management – page 3
Hodder Gibson Study Skills Advice – General – page 6
2015 EXAM – page 9
2016 EXAM (including replacement Question 1) – page 19
2017 EXAM – page 27
2017 SPECIMEN QUESTION PAPER – page 35
ANSWERS – page 45

EAST AYRSHIRE LEISURE TRUST	
541179	
Bertrams	18/01/2018
658.007	£9.99
	DI

HODDER GIBSON
AN HACHETTE UK COMPANY

This book contains the official SQA 2015, 2016 and 2017 Exams, and the 2017 Specimen Question Paper for National 5 Business Management, with associated SQA-approved answers modified from the official marking instructions that accompany the paper.

In addition the book contains study skills advice. This has been specially commissioned by Hodder Gibson, and has been written by experienced senior teachers and examiners in line with the new National 5 syllabus and assessment outlines. This is not SQA material but has been devised to provide further guidance for National 5 examinations.

Hodder Gibson is grateful to the copyright holders, as credited on the final page of the book, for permission to use their material.
Every effort has been made to trace the copyright holders and to obtain their permission for the use of copyright material. Hodder Gibson will be happy to receive information allowing us to rectify any error or omission in future editions.

Hachette UK's policy is to use papers that are natural, renewable and recyclable products and made from wood grown in sustainable forests. The logging and manufacturing processes are expected to conform to the environmental regulations of the country of origin.

Orders: please contact Bookpoint Ltd, 130 Park Drive, Milton Park, Abingdon, Oxon OX14 4SE. Telephone: (44) 01235 827720. Fax: (44) 01235 400454. Lines are open 9.00–5.00, Monday to Saturday, with a 24-hour message answering service. Visit our website at www.hoddereducation.co.uk.
Hodder Gibson can be contacted direct on: Tel: 0141 333 4650; Fax: 0141 404 8188; email: hoddergibson@hodder.co.uk

This collection first published in 2017 by
Hodder Gibson, an imprint of Hodder Education,
An Hachette UK Company
211 St Vincent Street
Glasgow G2 5QY

National 5 2015, 2016 and 2017 Exam Papers and Answers; 2017 Specimen Question Paper and Answers © Scottish Qualifications Authority. Study Skills section © Hodder Gibson. All rights reserved. Apart from any use permitted under UK copyright law, no part of this publication may be reproduced or transmitted in any form or by any means, electronic or mechanical, including photocopying and recording, or held within any information storage and retrieval system, without permission in writing from the publisher or under licence from the Copyright Licensing Agency Limited. Further details of such licences (for reprographic reproduction) may be obtained from the Copyright Licensing Agency Limited, www.cla.co.uk

Typeset by Aptara, Inc.

Printed in the UK

A catalogue record for this title is available from the British Library

ISBN: 978-1-5104-2158-5

2 1

2018 2017

Introduction

National 5 Business Management

This book of SQA past papers contains the question papers used in the 2016 and 2017 exams (with answers at the back of the book). The National 5 Business exam is being extended by 20 marks for 2018 onwards, following the removal of unit assessments from the course. A new specimen question paper, which reflects the requirements of the revised exam, is also included. The specimen question paper reflects the content and duration of the exam in 2018.

All of the question papers included in the book (2016, 2017 and the new specimen question paper) provide excellent representative exam practice for the final exams. Using the 2016 and 2017 past papers as part of your revision will help you to develop the vital skills and techniques needed for the exam, and will help you to identify any knowledge gaps you may have.

It is always a very good idea to refer to SQA's website for the most up-to-date course specification documents. These are available for each subject at www.sqa.org.uk/nqsubjects

The course

The National 5 Business Management course should enable you to develop:

- knowledge and understanding of the ways in which society relies on business to satisfy our needs
- an insight into the systems that organisations use to ensure customers' needs are met
- enterprising skills and attributes by providing you with opportunities to explore realistic business situations
- financial awareness through business contexts
- an insight into how organisations organise their resources for maximum efficiency and to improve their overall performance
- an awareness of how external influences impact on organisations.

The course is split into the following areas of study. The final exam can include questions on any of these areas.

- Understanding business
- Management of marketing
- Management of operations
- Management of people
- Management of finance

How the course is graded

The grade you achieve at the end of the National 5 Business Management course depends on two assessments:

- Assignment – this is submitted to SQA before your exam and counts for 25% of your final grade
- Exam – this counts for 75% of your final grade.

The course assessment for Session 2017/18 onwards

Question Paper

The Question Paper is now worth 90 marks (previously 70 marks) and contributes to 75% of your overall grade awarded for the Course.

Section 1 comprises 40 marks in total. This is made up of two pieces of stimulus material and questions of 20 marks each. The stimulus may be in the form of text, diagrams, financial information or graphs. The questions will be associated with the stimulus material and you should try, where possible, to relate your answers to the material provided. It will be based on real organisations. The questions can be drawn from any area of the course and will focus on decision making and the application of knowledge and understanding. Each question is broken down into sub-questions and the marks for each sub-question will range between 1–5 marks.

Section 2 comprises 50 marks in total. This is made up of five questions of 10 marks each. The questions can be drawn from any area of the course and will focus on the application of knowledge and understanding. The marks for each question in Section 2 will range between 1–4 marks.

You must attempt all questions in the question paper and it must be completed within 2 hours. The question paper is marked by SQA.

Assignment

The Assignment is worth 30 marks and contributes to 25% of your overall grade awarded for the Course.

The assignment gives you the opportunity to demonstrate your ability to:

- select an appropriate business topic.
- research and gather suitable business data/information/evidence relating to the context of the topic, from a range of sources.
- apply knowledge and understanding of business concepts to explain and analyse the key features of the topic.
- draw valid conclusions and/or recommendations to make informed business judgements and/or decisions.
- produce an appropriately formatted business report suitable for the purpose, intended audience and context of the assignment.

You will be given up to 5 hours in which to research and write up your final report before submitting it to SQA for marking. You must complete the assignment on your own, although your teacher will be able to give you some assistance in line with the guidance provided by SQA. This is an opportunity for you to gain valuable marks for your own piece of work.

Marks for the assignment are awarded for the following areas:

- background information – 4 marks
- research methods and sources – 6 marks
- findings, analysis and interpretation – 12 marks
- conclusion(s)/recommendation(s) – 6 marks
- collating and reporting – 2 marks

Your final report should be no longer than 1,300 words (excluding appendices). If the word count exceeds the maximum by more than 10%, a penalty will be applied when it is marked. There should be no more than two pages of appendices attached to your report.

Command words

It is often the case that candidates in the exam misunderstand what the question is asking them as they don't realise the importance of what is called the "Command Word". For example, if a question asks you to **identify** something, you only need to say what it is. However, if the question asks you to **describe** it, then you need to give some of the main features.

Example 1

Question: ***Identify*** *a source of finance for a business.* ***1 mark***

Acceptable answer: *A source of finance could be a Bank Loan.*

This answer will receive a mark as it does what the command word **identify** has asked.

Example 2

Question: ***Describe*** *a source of finance for a business.* ***1 mark***

Acceptable answer: *A loan from a bank which can be repaid with interest, over a period of time.*

In this case, where the command word is **describe**, there would be no marks awarded for the answer given in Example 1. You need to include some features of a bank loan (describe it) in order to get the mark. Remember, it is good practice to always answer in sentences.

So make sure you read the question carefully, checking the command word to see how you need to write your answer.

Context

Section 1 questions in the exam will provide you with a short piece of stimulus material, sometimes called a case study, with information about a small or medium sized business. The questions that follow will mostly relate to the case study and your answers should reflect the context given.

For example, if the case study is about a charity, then your answers should relate to a charity.

Example 3

Question: ***Give*** *an objective for the RSPCA.* ***1 mark***

Acceptable answer: *To promote animal welfare.*

Because the RSPCA is a charity there are a number of objectives that would not be suitable for them. For example, you would get no marks for saying an objective would be to make as much profit as possible.

Remember to relate all your answers to the business or organisation from the case study.

Marks

Check the number of marks for each question. Too often candidates write too much or too little. If there is only one mark available then you only need to make one point. It might be safer to give two just in case, but only if you have time. If there are four marks available, then you need to make four points to get full marks.

Check to make sure that you have made enough points in your answer to get full marks.

Topic areas

Understanding Business and Marketing are areas where candidates normally do well in exams. However, Finance proves tricky for a lot of students, and, to a lesser extent, so do Human Resources and Operations. There is no way to avoid questions on these topics, so you will need to learn what is contained in each.

Management of finance

There are only five parts to finance: sources of finance, break-even, cash budgeting, income statement and technology.

For sources of finance you only need to be aware of where the organisation can get money from. Remember, this can be either to invest in the business or to overcome a cash flow problem, so make sure you understand which you should write about, as the acceptable answers may be different for different questions.

For break-even, you need to memorise the formula for calculating contribution and break-even. Once you have done this, these questions should be fairly straightforward. Don't be put off by the use of numbers. The calculations you may be asked to carry out are relatively simple and you will be able to use a calculator.

When looking at cash budgets in a question, it is always better to read left to right rather than up and down. Look for trends, such as a source of income going down, or a cost that is increasing. These would show potential problems which the business should worry about.

Management of people

Candidates often confuse what is included under each heading for recruitment and selection.

- **Recruitment**

  It is generally accepted that the recruitment stage involves job analysis, job description, person specification, the decision about whether to recruit internally or externally, and, finally, the advertisement of the job.

- **Selection**

  Here you will be expected to give answers about selection methods. These could include application forms/CVs, references, interviews and the various forms of testing available.

  Remember that the recruitment stage is about the job and the selection stage is about picking the right person!

Management of operations

The main problem encountered by candidates is what is meant by quality. There are only two methods you need to know about.

- **Quality control**

  This is a simple system where the quality of raw materials is checked at the start of production, and the quality of the finished product is checked at the end.

- **Quality management**

  Here quality is checked at every stage from carrying out market research to learn what the customers need from the product, to providing quality after-sales service.

Problem answers

Some of the answers you might give to a question are not suitable for gaining marks. Try not to use answers such as "quicker", "easier", "more efficient", "saves time", "saves money" as these do not attract marks. They are *relative terms* and if you do use them you must show what you are comparing them to.

Example 4

Question: ***Outline*** *an advantage of using spreadsheets in Finance.* ***1 mark***

Acceptable answer: *Formulas in the spreadsheet will carry out calculations automatically.*

You would not get a mark for saying it is faster than doing calculations by hand.

Always use business terminology in your answers – this is far more likely to get you the marks!

Good luck!

A lot of what you will learn in National 5 Business Management is common sense. As a consumer and a member of society you are already aware of most of the course content. The challenge is to make sure you understand the terms used. Hard work and good preparation go a long way, so keep calm and don't panic! GOOD LUCK!

Study Skills – what you need to know to pass exams!

Pause for thought

Many students might skip quickly through a page like this. After all, we all know how to revise. Do you really though?

Think about this:

"IF YOU ALWAYS DO WHAT YOU ALWAYS DO, YOU WILL ALWAYS GET WHAT YOU HAVE ALWAYS GOT."

Do you like the grades you get? Do you want to do better? If you get full marks in your assessment, then that's great! Change nothing! This section is just to help you get that little bit better than you already are.

There are two main parts to the advice on offer here. The first part highlights fairly obvious things but which are also very important. The second part makes suggestions about revision that you might not have thought about but which WILL help you.

Part 1

DOH! It's so obvious but …

Start revising in good time

Don't leave it until the last minute – this will make you panic.

Make a revision timetable that sets out work time AND play time.

Sleep and eat!

Obvious really, and very helpful. Avoid arguments or stressful things too – even games that wind you up. You need to be fit, awake and focused!

Know your place!

Make sure you know exactly **WHEN and WHERE** your exams are.

Know your enemy!

Make sure you know what to expect in the exam.

How is the paper structured?

How much time is there for each question?

What types of question are involved?

Which topics seem to come up time and time again?

Which topics are your strongest and which are your weakest?

Are all topics compulsory or are there choices?

Learn by DOING!

There is no substitute for past papers and practice papers – they are simply essential! Tackling this collection of papers and answers is exactly the right thing to be doing as your exams approach.

Part 2

People learn in different ways. Some like low light, some bright. Some like early morning, some like evening / night. Some prefer warm, some prefer cold. But everyone uses their BRAIN and the brain works when it is active. Passive learning – sitting gazing at notes – is the most INEFFICIENT way to learn anything. Below you will find tips and ideas for making your revision more effective and maybe even more enjoyable. What follows gets your brain active, and active learning works!

Activity 1 – Stop and review

Step 1

When you have done no more than 5 minutes of revision reading STOP!

Step 2

Write a heading in your own words which sums up the topic you have been revising.

Step 3

Write a summary of what you have revised in no more than two sentences. Don't fool yourself by saying, "I know it, but I cannot put it into words". That just means you don't know it well enough. If you cannot write your summary, revise that section again, knowing that you must write a summary at the end of it. Many of you will have notebooks full of blue/black ink writing. Many of the pages will not be especially attractive or memorable so try to liven them up a bit with colour as you are reviewing and rewriting. **This is a great memory aid, and memory is the most important thing.**

Activity 2 – Use technology!

Why should everything be written down? Have you thought about "mental" maps, diagrams, cartoons and colour to help you learn? And rather than write down notes, why not record your revision material?

What about having a text message revision session with friends? Keep in touch with them to find out how and what they are revising and share ideas and questions.

Why not make a video diary where you tell the camera what you are doing, what you think you have learned and what you still have to do? No one has to see or hear it, but the process of having to organise your thoughts in a formal way to explain something is a very important learning practice.

Be sure to make use of electronic files. You could begin to summarise your class notes. Your typing might be slow, but it will get faster and the typed notes will be easier to read than the scribbles in your class notes. Try to add different fonts and colours to make your work stand out. You can easily Google relevant pictures, cartoons and diagrams which you can copy and paste to make your work more attractive and **MEMORABLE**.

Activity 3 – This is it. Do this and you will know lots!

Step 1

In this task you must be very honest with yourself! Find the SQA syllabus for your subject (www.sqa.org.uk). Look at how it is broken down into main topics called MANDATORY knowledge. That means stuff you MUST know.

Step 2

BEFORE you do ANY revision on this topic, write a list of everything that you already know about the subject. It might be quite a long list but you only need to write it once. It shows you all the information that is already in your long-term memory so you know what parts you do not need to revise!

Step 3

Pick a chapter or section from your book or revision notes. Choose a fairly large section or a whole chapter to get the most out of this activity.

With a buddy, use Skype, Facetime, Twitter or any other communication you have, to play the game "If this is the answer, what is the question?". For example, if you are revising Geography and the answer you provide is "meander", your buddy would have to make up a question like "What is the word that describes a feature of a river where it flows slowly and bends often from side to side?".

Make up 10 "answers" based on the content of the chapter or section you are using. Give this to your buddy to solve while you solve theirs.

Step 4

Construct a wordsearch of at least 10 × 10 squares. You can make it as big as you like but keep it realistic. Work together with a group of friends. Many apps allow you to make wordsearch puzzles online. The words and phrases can go in any direction and phrases can be split. Your puzzle must only contain facts linked to the topic you are revising. Your task is to find 10 bits of information to hide in your puzzle, but you must not repeat information that you used in Step 3. DO NOT show where the words are. Fill up empty squares with random letters. Remember to keep a note of where your answers are hidden but do not show your friends. When you have a complete puzzle, exchange it with a friend to solve each other's puzzle.

Step 5

Now make up 10 questions (not "answers" this time) based on the same chapter used in the previous two tasks. Again, you must find NEW information that you have not yet used. Now it's getting hard to find that new information! Again, give your questions to a friend to answer.

Step 6

As you have been doing the puzzles, your brain has been actively searching for new information. Now write a NEW LIST that contains only the new information you have discovered when doing the puzzles. Your new list is the one to look at repeatedly for short bursts over the next few days. Try to remember more and more of it without looking at it. After a few days, you should be able to add words from your second list to your first list as you increase the information in your long-term memory.

FINALLY! Be inspired...

Make a list of different revision ideas and beside each one write **THINGS I HAVE** tried, **THINGS I WILL** try and **THINGS I MIGHT** try. Don't be scared of trying something new.

And remember – "FAIL TO PREPARE AND PREPARE TO FAIL!"

NATIONAL 5

2015

N5 National Qualifications 2015

X710/75/11

Business Management

MONDAY, 11 MAY

1:00 PM — 2:30 PM

Total marks — 70

SECTION 1 — 30 marks

Attempt BOTH questions.

SECTION 2 — 40 marks

Attempt ALL questions.

Write your answers clearly in the answer booklet provided. In the answer booklet you must clearly identify the question number you are attempting.

Use **blue** or **black** ink.

You may use a calculator.

Before leaving the examination room you must give your answer booklet to the Invigilator; if you do not, you may lose all the marks for this paper.

MARKS

SECTION 1 — 30 marks

Attempt BOTH questions

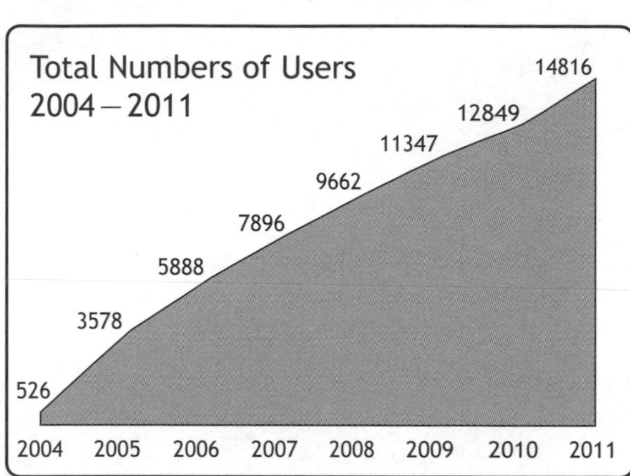

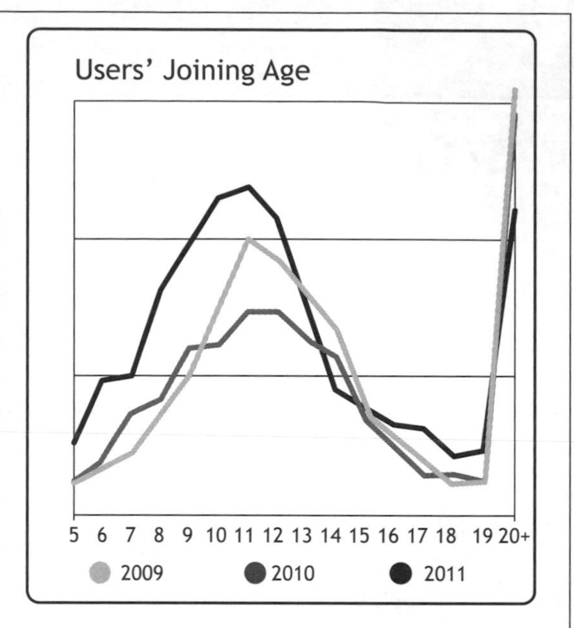

The Factory Skatepark, based in Dundee, was recently named Social Enterprise of the Year. It offers extreme sports, youth and homework clubs, IT classes for the elderly and photography classes. It also has a sports shop and cafe.

The organisation is supported by grants from organisations including the People's Postcode Lottery, Comic Relief and the Big Lottery Fund. A major sponsor is Rockstar Energy drinks which is a favourite choice amongst teenage customers.

Factory Skatepark uses its website and social media to give information to customers and has launched an app to let members book sessions. Members are encouraged to give feedback to the organisation to help it meet its aims of improving customer service and finding interesting activities for all users.

You should note that although the following questions are based on the case study above, you will need to make use of knowledge and understanding you have gained whilst studying the Course.

1. (a) From the case study, identify **2** market segments that the organisation is targeting. **2**

   (b) (i) From the case study, identify a charitable organisation that supports Factory Skatepark. **1**

   (ii) Identify the sector of the economy that a charity would operate in. **1**

   (iii) Describe **one** other sector of the economy. **1**

   (c) Describe the features of a social enterprise. **2**

   (d) (i) Outline the ways in which the skatepark can gain customer feedback. **2**

   (ii) Explain the benefits of good customer service to the skatepark. **2**

MARKS

1. (continued)

(e) (i) From the case study, identify the ways in which technology is used in promoting the skatepark. **2**

(ii) Describe the benefits of using technology to promote the skatepark. **2**

[Turn over

MARKS

Glasgow-based clothing manufacturer Trespass was proud to be the official casual uniform supplier to the 2014 Commonwealth Games. The business is run by brothers Afzal and Akmal Khushi who established the Trespass brand in 1984. The business is run as a private limited company.

The owners were pleased to mark the 30th anniversary of the brand with such an honour. They have a wide range of products for men, women and children and specialise in sportswear for active pursuits. Customers can buy products online as well as in Trespass stores and outdoor clothing suppliers such as Go Outdoors.

Trespass mass-produces its clothing and uses hi-tech production. This ensures that quality is a key focus. The company has stores worldwide and employs hundreds of staff. Trespass prides itself in having a happy workforce and provides an excellent training programme for staff.

GLASGOW 2014
XX COMMONWEALTH GAMES

You should note that although the following questions are based on the case study above, you will need to make use of knowledge and understanding you have gained whilst studying the Course.

2. (a) From the case study, identify a sector of industry in which Trespass operates. **1**

(b) Describe the features of a private limited company. **2**

(c) Explain the benefits to a business of having a strong brand. **2**

(d) (i) From the case study, describe the method of production used. **1**

(ii) Discuss the costs and benefits of using this method of production. **3**

(e) Describe the methods that can be used to train employees in the business. **3**

(f) Describe the interests of stakeholders identified in the case study. **3**

[Turn over for SECTION 2 on *Page six*

DO NOT WRITE ON THIS PAGE

MARKS

SECTION 2 — 40 marks

Attempt ALL questions

3. Maddy Taylor is the owner and only employee of a cake-making business called Charm Cakes. She has produced the following break-even chart based on sales of her standard cakes.

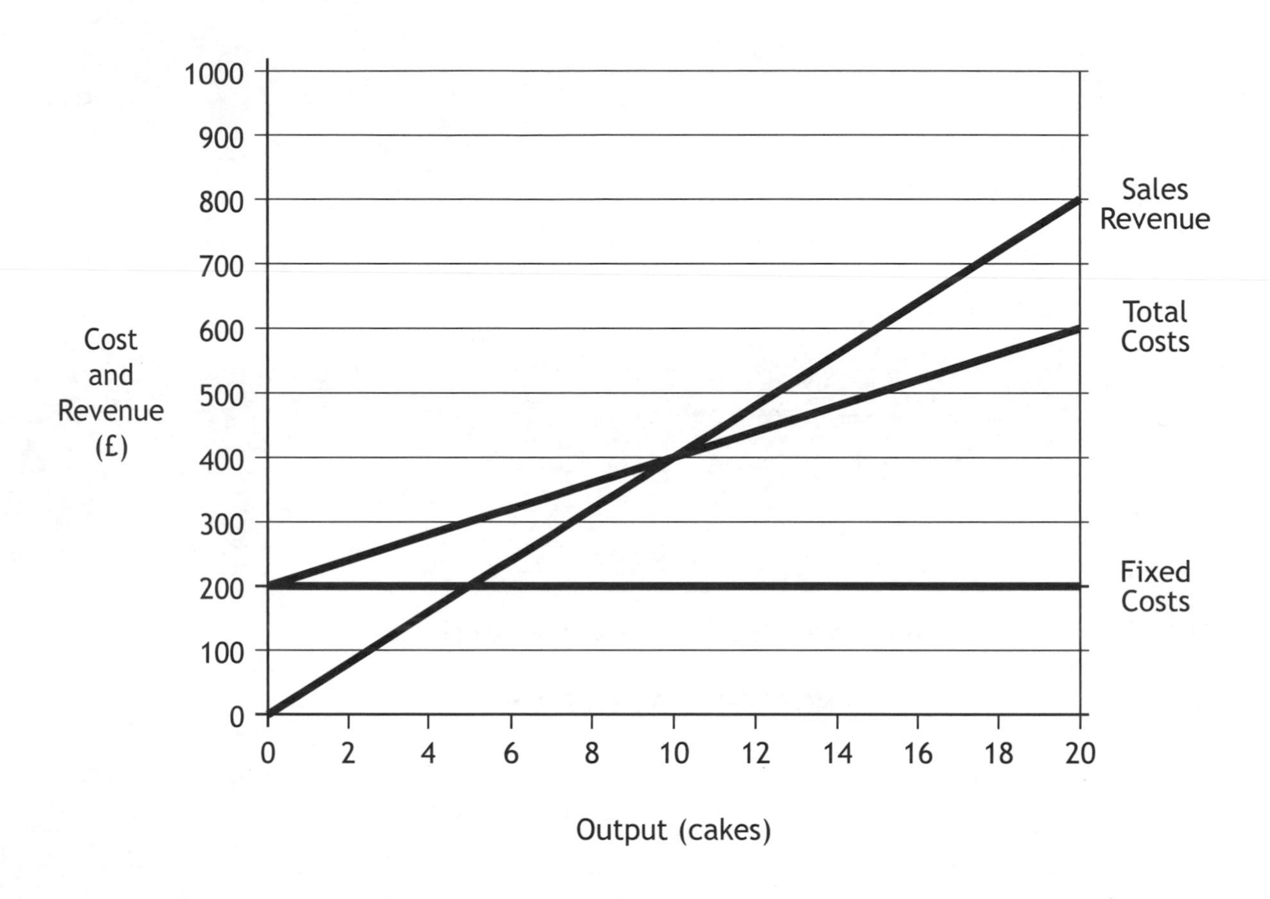

(a) From the break even chart, identify:

- the number of cakes sold at the Break-Even Point;
- Total Costs at Break-Even Point. **2**

(b) From the chart, calculate the Variable Cost per Unit. **2**

(c) Define the following terms.

- Break-Even
- Fixed Costs
- Variable Costs **3**

(d) Justify the use of the following sources of finance:

- a bank loan;
- a grant;
- an overdraft. **3**

			MARKS
4.	(a)	Describe stages of the recruitment process.	**4**
	(b)	Outline the role of technology when recruiting and selecting staff.	**3**
	(c)	Describe the responsibilities of the employer under Health and Safety legislation.	**3**
5.	(a)	Describe the advantages of computerised stock control.	**3**
	(b)	Describe how an operations department can be environmentally friendly.	**2**
	(c)	(i) Identify **2** quality inputs in the production process.	**2**
		(ii) Justify the importance of using good quality inputs in the production process.	**3**
6.	(a)	Promotion is an element of the marketing mix.	
		(i) Describe the other elements of the marketing mix.	**3**
		(ii) Outline the methods of sales promotion which an organisation could use.	**3**
	(b)	Discuss the costs and benefits of using desk research.	**4**

[END OF QUESTION PAPER]

[BLANK PAGE]

DO NOT WRITE ON THIS PAGE

NATIONAL 5

2016

X710/75/11 **Business Management**

FRIDAY, 27 MAY

9:00 AM – 10:30 AM

Total marks — 70

SECTION 1 — 30 marks

Attempt BOTH questions.

SECTION 2 — 40 marks

Attempt ALL questions.

Write your answers clearly in the answer booklet provided. In the answer booklet you must clearly identify the question number you are attempting.

Use **blue** or **black** ink.

You may use a calculator.

Before leaving the examination room you must give your answer booklet to the Invigilator; if you do not, you may lose all the marks for this paper.

©

MARKS

SECTION 1 — 30 marks

Attempt BOTH questions

Question 1 of this paper replaces the original one in the SQA Past Paper 2016, which cannot be reproduced for copyright reasons. As such, it should be stressed that it is not an official SQA-verified section, although every care has been taken by the Publishers to ensure that it offers appropriate practice material for National 5 Business Management.

Just Dogs

Just Dogs was established in December 2006 by Gemma Johnstone. As a devoted dog owner and dog lover Gemma wanted to offer "doggy" people the chance to visit a shop that would offer a great selection of quality and unique dog accessories and supplies. Whilst the online doggy market proves popular, Gemma wanted to give dog owners the opportunity to be able to visit the shop, see the products and try them out before purchasing. Gemma also likes to be on hand to offer advice and tips to customers who visit the shop, which is based in Edinburgh.

Gemma is currently studying towards the Advanced Diploma in Canine Behaviour. This means that she is able to provide competent advice regarding dog training, behaviour and nutrition. It is important to Gemma to be able to offer a personal, tailored service to customers and this is central to the way the business is operated.

Just Dogs promotes responsible dog ownership. All of its practical doggy products are accompanied with useful guidance, tips and messages. This allows owners to look after their dogs in the best possible manner.

Adapted from www.justdogsshop.co.uk

You should note that although the following questions are based on the case study above, you will need to make use of knowledge and understanding you have gained whilst studying the Course.

1. (a) (i) From the case study, identify the type of business that Gemma operates. **1**

(ii) Using information from the case study and knowledge that you have gained, give 2 examples of good customer service. **2**

(b) Describe 2 costs and 2 benefits to Gemma of operating a website as well as her shop. **4**

(c) Outline methods of promotion that Gemma could use for her business. **3**

(d) Gemma is undertaking training to help her provide a better service to her customers.

Describe the benefits of staff training. **3**

(e) Describe 2 costs that Gemma may have in her business. **2**

MARKS

WHO MADE YOUR PANTS?

Who Made Your Pants? is an ethical business that was launched in 2008 by Becky John because she really didn't like wearing clothes that were made in sweatshop conditions. The company makes underwear using traditional fabrics, like lycra and lace, which are bought from big underwear companies. These fabrics are unwanted materials which are normally thrown out as waste at the end of a season.

In 2014, Becky won Social Entrepreneur of the Year for her business that creates manufacturing jobs for women who have been excluded due to their status as refugees. She employs 8 women with refugee backgrounds from countries such as Sudan, Somalia and Afghanistan.

The company provides training and every new recruit starts by working on one style of underwear and then moves onto the more complicated styles. The pants are handmade and each woman has a specialist job like cutting, sewing or trimming so there will always be more than one person involved in the making of each piece of underwear. All profits the company makes go back into the business.

You should note that although the following questions are based on the case study above, you will need to make use of knowledge and understanding you have gained whilst studying the Course.

2. (a) (i) From the case study, identify **one** way that Who Made Your Pants is ethical in its production. 1

(ii) Justify the importance of ethical production. 3

(b) Who Made Your Pants sells its products online.

Explain the benefits of online selling (e-commerce). 3

(c) (i) Identify **one** type of training used by Who Made Your Pants. 1

(ii) Describe an advantage of the type of training identified in (c)(i). 1

(d) Describe the methods of selection that could be used by Who Made Your Pants. 3

(e) Describe the methods that Who Made Your Pants could use to ensure the quality of its underwear. 3

[Turn over

MARKS

SECTION 2 — 40 marks
Attempt ALL questions

3. (a) Internal factors can influence performance.
   (i) Identify **2** internal factors. 2
   (ii) Explain the influence of the factors identified in (a)(i). 2

   (b) Outline the objectives of a non-profit-making organisation. 2

   (c) Discuss the advantages and disadvantages of operating as a sole trader. 4

4. (a) Outline the ways an organisation could use the following technology in the recruitment and selection process.
   (i) Word processing package 1
   (ii) Database package 1
   (iii) Company website 1

   (b) (i) Identify **2** methods of industrial action. 2
   (ii) Explain the impact of industrial action. 3

   (c) Outline the impact of technology on working practices. 2

[Turn over

MARKS

5. Cash Budget for Green Energy Solutions Ltd

	£ May	£ June	£ July
OPENING BALANCE	20,000	(3,000)	(2,000)
RECEIPTS			
Sales Revenue	2,000	8,000	13,000
TOTAL	22,000	5,000	11,000
PAYMENTS			
Purchases	1,000	2,000	3,500
Wages	3,000	4,000	4,000
Advertising	1,000	1,000	1,000
Purchase of Motor Van	20,000	0	0
TOTAL	25,000	7,000	8,500
CLOSING BALANCE	**(3,000)**	**(2,000)**	**2,500**

(a) (i) From the cash budget, identify **2** cash flow problems. **2**

(ii) Describe how the problems identified in part (a)(i) could be solved. **4**

(b) From the cash budget, identify an example of:

(i) a fixed cost; **1**

(ii) a variable cost. **1**

(c) Outline the purposes of producing an income statement. **2**

6. (a) Describe the methods of production. **3**

(b) Outline the factors an organisation might consider when choosing a supplier. **3**

(c) Explain the possible problems of:

- under-stocking;
- over-stocking. **4**

[END OF QUESTION PAPER]

[BLANK PAGE]

DO NOT WRITE ON THIS PAGE

NATIONAL 5

2017

National
Qualifications
2017

X710/75/11 **Business Management**

TUESDAY, 16 MAY
9:00 AM – 10:30 AM

Total marks — 70

SECTION 1 — 30 marks

Attempt BOTH questions.

SECTION 2 — 40 marks

Attempt ALL questions.

Write your answers clearly in the answer booklet provided. In the answer booklet you must clearly identify the question number you are attempting.

Use **blue** or **black** ink.

You may use a calculator.

Before leaving the examination room you must give your answer booklet to the Invigilator; if you do not, you may lose all the marks for this paper.

©

MARKS

SECTION 1 — 30 marks

Attempt BOTH questions

Charles MacLeod's famous Stornoway Black Pudding can be found on menus in restaurants all over the UK. It has also featured in many restaurant reviews in newspapers. Charles MacLeod Ltd is a family run butcher that prides itself on its customer satisfaction.

The business makes the famous black pudding by hand in its premises on the Isle of Lewis under strict UK health and safety food production regulations. "Stornoway Black Pudding" is a term that is protected by European Union legislation which states it must be made in Stornoway. Rivals therefore cannot use the name "Stornoway" in their brand.

The distinctive MacLeod tartan design makes its shop premises stand out in Stornoway. Due to the high demand for the puddings, the business rarely needs to advertise; however they use a well-designed website and social media to communicate with customers.

You should note that although the following questions are based on the case study above, you will need to make use of knowledge and understanding you have gained whilst studying the Course.

1. (a) (i) From the case study, identify the methods used to promote the business. **2**

   (ii) Explain the benefits of branding to the business. **3**

   (b) (i) State a suitable method that could be used to distribute the products to butchers across the UK. **1**

   (ii) Discuss the costs and benefits of using the method of distribution stated in (b)(i). **3**

   (c) From the case study, describe the effect of external factors on the business. **3**

   (d) Compare the features of a private limited company to a sole trader. **3**

MARKS

The owners of iQ Superfood Chocolate, based in Stirling, have taken advantage of the recent growth in the market for organic foods by introducing a range of healthy chocolate products.

iQ has come up with a delicious chocolate range, which contains super food nutrients and antioxidants. Bars have less than 199 calories with a taste to delight chocolate-lovers and the health-conscious alike. The business has also produced new "BeautiQ" and "YogiQ" bars which it claims are specifically beneficial to the skin and health. iQ is particular to ensure that it, along with its suppliers, plays its part in ethical sourcing and distribution.

The bars can be bought in independent retailers and health centres but the business aims to have these products stocked in all the major retailers in the UK.

You should note that although the following questions are based on the case study above, you will need to make use of knowledge and understanding you have gained whilst studying the Course.

2. (a) (i) From the case study, identify the markets targeted by iQ. 2

(ii) Outline the benefits of target marketing for a business. 3

(b) (i) Describe a suitable method of production for making iQ products. 1

(ii) Discuss the costs and benefits of using the method of production described in (b)(i). 3

(c) Describe the costs and benefits of having an ethical approach to sourcing and distribution of products. 3

(d) Explain how stakeholders identified in the case study can influence the business. 3

[Turn over

MARKS

SECTION 2 — 40 marks

Attempt ALL questions

3. (a) (i) Identify **2** sectors of the economy. 2

(ii) Compare the objectives of the sectors identified in (a)(i). 2

(b) Describe **3** methods of ensuring good customer service. 3

(c) Explain how internal factors could influence the success of the organisation. 3

4. (a) Describe the documents that could be used in the recruitment process. 3

(b) Compare the use of internal and external methods of recruitment. 2

(c) Explain the benefits of training employees. 3

(d) Outline the features of the Equality Act. 2

5. (a) Describe the types of technology which could be used within the operations function. 4

(b) (i) Describe the methods that an organisation could use to ensure the quality of its finished goods. 4

(ii) Define the following terms:

- Maximum inventory (stock) level
- Lead time. 2

MARKS

6. John McLean is a sole trader who operates a small business. He has produced the following Income Statement for Year 2.

Income Statement for John McLean
For the year ended 31 December Year 2

	£	£
A		70,000
Less Cost of Sales		40,000
Gross Profit		B
Less Expenses		
Electricity	1,000	
Rent	4,000	
Wages	5,000	
		10,000
PROFIT FOR THE YEAR		C

(a) From the Income Statement, complete the missing information for entries **A**, **B** and **C**. 3

(b) (i) Describe the sources of finance available to a private limited company for expansion. 2

(ii) Justify the use of sources of finance outlined in (b)(i). (A different justification should be given for each source.) 3

(c) Outline the benefits of budgeting to an organisation. 2

[END OF QUESTION PAPER]

[BLANK PAGE]

DO NOT WRITE ON THIS PAGE

NATIONAL 5

2017 Specimen Question Paper

N5

National Qualifications
SPECIMEN ONLY

S810/75/11 **Business Management**

Date — Not applicable

Duration — 2 hours

Total marks — 90

SECTION 1 — 40 marks

Attempt BOTH questions.

SECTION 2 — 50 marks

Attempt ALL questions.

Write your answers clearly in the answer booklet provided. In the answer booklet you must clearly identify the question number you are attempting.

Use **blue** or **black** ink.

You may use a calculator.

Before leaving the examination room you must give your answer booklet to the Invigilator; if you do not, you may lose all the marks for this paper.

©

SECTION 1 — 40 marks

Attempt BOTH questions

Background

Cuddybridge is a small producer of apple juice based in the Scottish Borders. The company began by producing cider in 2007 but soon realised that there was too much competition in the market from large brands and decided it was more profitable to produce apple juice.

Production

All the apples are hand pressed and no artificial flavourings, colourings or E-numbers are added. Cuddybridge tries to press the apples as soon as they are received, so that customers get the freshest juice possible.

The company uses more than 15,000 kilograms of apples per week, 365 days of the year, so relying on Scottish apples alone is not an option. Cuddybridge is aware that importing apples increases its carbon footprint. In order to be environmentally friendly it sends all its waste squashed apples to become animal feed for two types of rare breed pigs.

Cuddybridge's client list continues to increase and it now sells to cafes, delis and restaurants around the Borders. It has also recently started to supply top-named restaurants in Edinburgh as well as the famous department store Harvey Nichols. It has won many awards including Scotland Food and Drink Excellence Awards.

The top three product trends with fast paced growth:

Vegetable Nutrition - New products with vegetables as an ingredient have seen 43% growth rate between 2012 and 2015

All Natural - 67% of consumers rated "all natural" as the most interesting product attribute

Speciality 100% Juice - 60% globally say they are interested in products with proven health benefits

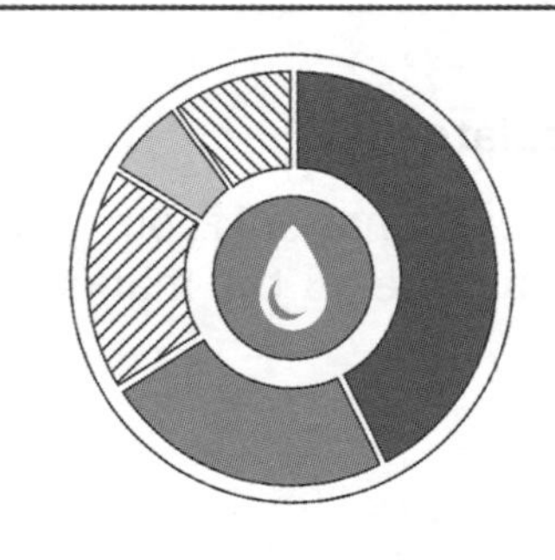

UK soft drinks sectors

- Carbonates (43%)
- Dilutables (23%)
- Bottled water (18%)
- Fruit juice (6%)
- Still and juice drinks (10%)

MARKS

The following questions are based on the case study. You will need to make use of knowledge and understanding you have gained whilst studying the course.

1. (a) (i) From the case study, identify **one** way that Cuddybridge is ethical in its production. 1

(ii) Justify the importance of ethical production. 3

(b) Compare job production with flow production. 3

(c) (i) Using the case study, identify reasons why Cuddybridge started producing apple juice. 2

(ii) Explain how external factors could affect the success of Cuddybridge. 5

(d) Describe methods that Cuddybridge could use to ensure the quality of its apple juice. 3

(e) (i) Identify a suitable method of distribution for Cuddybridge Apple Juice. 1

(ii) Justify the method identified in (e)(i). 2

MARKS

It has been more than 10 years since Jamie Oliver opened his Fifteen restaurant in London as a social enterprise, which was followed on a Channel 4 documentary called Jamie's Kitchen.

Jamie had the vision of creating one of London's finest restaurants and using the magic of cooking to give young people who have faced enormous challenges in their lives the opportunity to unlock their true talent through providing great training and mentoring. The year-long apprenticeship consisted of working alongside top chefs in the restaurant and also spending time at college.

To apply for the apprenticeship applicants had to be between 16 and 24 and not be in employment, education or training. In the first year there were over 300 applications for just 21 places.

All profits from the restaurants are donated to The Jamie Oliver Food Foundation which is a charity that aims to teach people about food, where it comes from, how it affects their bodies and how to cook it.

£1.20

The Daily News

CITY FINAL | Monday 20th February 2017 | VOL 32 NO.10

Rising Prices and Shrinking Products

Dispatches, a Channel 4 documentary, reported that after Brexit food prices in the UK were increasing, mainly due to the rising cost of raw materials from Europe. As a result the prices paid by consumers for restaurant meals has also increased.

Source: Channel4Dispatches - Supermarkets: Brexit & Your Shrinking Shop

MARKS

The following questions are based on the case study. You will need to make use of knowledge and understanding you have gained whilst studying the course.

				MARKS
2.	(a)	(i)	From the case study, identify a type of training used by Fifteen.	1
		(ii)	Discuss the advantages and disadvantages of the type of training identified in (a)(i).	3
	(b)		Describe methods of selection that could be used by Fifteen to select apprentices.	4
	(c)		Using the case study, compare the objectives of Fifteen with those of an organisation in the private sector.	3
	(d)		Explain the benefits to Fifteen of Jamie's celebrity endorsement.	3
	(e)		Describe how technology could be used in the marketing and operations functions of Fifteen.	3
	(f)		Outline ways that Fifteen could reduce costs.	3

MARKS

SECTION 2 — 50 marks

Attempt ALL questions

3. (a) (i) Identify **2** stakeholders of a private sector organisation. 2

(ii) Explain the impact that the stakeholders identified in (a)(i) could have on the organisation. 3

(b) Outline how an organisation could maximise customer satisfaction. 3

(c) Distinguish between a sole trader and a private limited company. 2

4. (a) (i) Outline the factors that would be considered before setting a price for a product. 3

(ii) Describe pricing strategies for a new product. 2

(b) Explain the benefits of branding. 3

(c) Describe how an organisation can be ethical in its marketing activities. 2

5. (a) Outline the stages of the recruitment process. 4

(b) Describe payment systems used to calculate employee wages. 4

(c) Identify **2** pieces of employment legislation. 2

MARKS

6. Cash Budget for Blooming Florist Ltd

	£ May	£ June	£ July
OPENING BALANCE	20,000	−3,000	−2,000
RECEIPTS			
Sales Revenue	2,000	(ii)	13,000
TOTAL	22,000	5,000	11,000
PAYMENTS			
Purchases	1,000	2,000	3,500
Wages	3,000	4,000	4,000
Advertising	1,000	1,000	1,000
Purchase of Motor Van	(i)	0	0
TOTAL	25,000	7,000	8,500
CLOSING BALANCE	**−3,000**	**−2,000**	**2,500**

(a) From the cash budget, calculate the missing figures (i) and (ii). **2**

(b) Discuss sources of finance that could be used by a private limited company. **4**

(c) Justify the use of spreadsheets in the Finance department. **2**

(d) Outline the purpose of producing an Income Statement. **2**

7. (a) Describe the factors that would be considered before choosing a supplier of raw materials. **4**

(b) Draw and label an inventory control diagram. **3**

(c) Explain the problems that could be encountered if an organisation:

- overstocks
- understocks. **3**

[END OF SPECIMEN QUESTION PAPER]

[BLANK PAGE]

DO NOT WRITE ON THIS PAGE

NATIONAL 5

Answers

ANSWERS FOR

SQA NATIONAL 5 BUSINESS MANAGEMENT 2017

NATIONAL 5 BUSINESS MANAGEMENT 2015

Questions that ask candidates to **Describe . . .**
Candidates must make a number of relevant, factual points up to the total mark allocation for the question. These should be key points. The points do not need to be in any particular order. Candidates may provide a number of straightforward points or a smaller number of developed points, or a combination of these.

Up to the total mark allocation for this question:
- 1 mark should be given for each accurate relevant point of knowledge.
- a second mark could be given for any point that is developed from the point of knowledge.

Questions that ask candidates to **Explain . . .**
Candidates must make a number of points that relate cause and effect and/or make the relationships between things clear, for example by showing connections between a process/situation. These should be key reasons and may include theoretical concepts. There is no need to prioritise the reasons.
Candidates may provide a number of straightforward reasons or a smaller number of developed reasons, or a combination of these.

Up to the total mark allocation for this question:
- 1 mark should be given for each accurate relevant point of reason.
- a second mark could be given for any other point that is developed from the same reason.

Questions that ask candidates to **Discuss . . .**
Where question asks candidates to discuss advantages and disadvantages they must make a number of relevant advantages and disadvantages up to the total mark allocation for the question. However, where question is only discuss this invites positives and negatives but does not insist on both.

Up to the total mark allocation for this question:
- 1 mark should be given for each advantage/disadvantage.

Section 1

1. (a) Identifiable market segments:
   - Age (only accept one example, e.g. youth)
   - Hobby/Interest
   - Location (Dundee)
   - Education

   (b) (i) Identifiable charitable organisations:
   - People's Postcode Lottery
   - Comic Relief
   - Big Lottery Fund

   (ii) Response should be:
   - Third
   - Voluntary

   (iii) Responses could include:

   Private Sector
   - Organisations owned by private individuals
   - Aim to make a profit

   Public Sector
   - Organisations owned and controlled by the government or local authorities
   - Financed by taxes

   (c) Responses could include:
   - Can be a profit making organisation
   - Uses its profits to help its cause
   - Primarily has social or environmental aims
   - Provide community benefits
   - Job creation
   - Funded by grants and sponsorship
   - Has employees and volunteers
   - Operates in the third/voluntary sector

   (d) (i) Responses could include:
   - Ask customers opinions/interview customers
   - Place suggestions box in centre
   - Post a survey/questionnaire to their home
   - Create a feedback section on website
   - Set up a focus group
   - Feedback form

   (ii) Responses could include:
   - Good customer recommendations which may lead to higher market share
   - Returning customers which increases sales/profits
   - Increased customer loyalty which makes it easier to promote new products
   - Improved reputation which attracts more customers or allows for higher prices to be charged
   - Improved customer satisfaction which means customers may return

   (e) (i) Identifiable methods of promotion:
   - Smartphone/Tablet app
   - Website
   - Social media, e.g. Facebook/Twitter

   (ii) Responses could include:
   - Allows for communication 24/7
   - Communication is possible all over the world
   - Communication is faster/instant
   - A more cost effective way of promoting the organisation
   - Can pass on large volumes of information through the website or e-mail
   - Can target potential customers more easily
   - Creates a good image for the target market

2. (a) Identifiable sector of industry:
   - Secondary sector
   - Tertiary sector

   (b) Responses could include:
   - A business which is owned by a shareholder(s)
   - Shares are not traded on the stock market/sold privately
   - Run by a board of directors
   - Incorporated – separate legal identity from owners
   - Limited liability for owners

   (c) Responses could include:
   - Brand loyalty which means you are guaranteed returning customers
   - Brand recognition so less advertising required
   - Gives an illusion/image of quality which means higher prices can be charged
   - Easier to launch new products due to customers being familiar with the brand

(d) (i) Identifiable methods of production:
- Flow production – products are made in stages on a production/assembly line
- Batch production – products are made in groups where one group of products are made together before another group is started

(ii) Responses could include:

Flow
- Fast rate of production
  - Allows organisation to cope with demand
- Manufacturing costs are reduced
  - Allows for more profits to be made
- Mechanisation/automation can be used
  - Fewer staff wages need to be paid
- Standardisation of products
  - Fewer complaints as all products are identical
- Economies of scale can be gained
  - Discounts from bulk buying would be possible
- Machine break-down can halt production
  - Leads to unhappy customers/loss of custom
- Lack of variety of products
  - Customers may not pay a premium price for mass produced goods

Batch
- Variety of products can be produced
  - Can meet customers specifications to a degree
- Economies of scale can be gained
- Mechanisation/automation can be used
- All products in batch are identical
- Equipment must be cleaned between batches
  - Slows production down

(e) Responses could include:
- Cascading – employees cascade training information to colleagues
- Role Play – acting out or demonstrating a role or scenario to provide a demonstration of how to perform under particular conditions
- Coaching – being taken through a task step by step and helped by a trainer or a coach
- Demonstration – trainee watches a task being demonstrated and then completes it themselves
- Induction training – new employees are trained when they first start in an organisation
  - Usually training on health and safety, procedures of the organisation
- On-the-job training – employees are trained in the workplace whilst carrying out the job
  - This could be done by shadowing a colleague
  - Employee learns the processes specific to the organisation
- Off-the-job training – employees are trained away from the workplace
  - This could be at a training centre or college
  - Employees are trained by experts

(f) Identifiable stakeholders are as follows. Responses could include:

Owners/Shareholders
- Level of profits they earn
- Image of the organisation
- Dividends/return on investment

Staff
- Level of pay
- Good working conditions
- Job security

Customers/Commonwealth Committee
- High quality products for best possible price/value for money
- Regular/consistent supply of goods
- Customer service provided

Section 2

3. (a) No. of cakes at BEP – 10 cakes
Total Costs at BEP – £400

(b) Variable Cost per Unit:
Total Costs – Fixed Costs = Variable Costs
£400 – £200 = £200
£200/10 units = £20 per unit

(c) Responses could include:

Break-Even
- Point at which Total Costs = Total Sales/Revenue
- Neither a Profit or a Loss is made as this is the point where sales cover costs

Fixed Costs
- Costs which do not vary with output or sales

Variable Costs
- Costs which vary directly with output or sales

(d) Responses could include:

Bank loan
- Paid back in instalments
- Paid over a long period of time

Grant
- Money does not need to be repaid

Overdraft
- Suitable for short-term cash flow problems
- Money available quickly as it can be prearranged
- Can take more money out than you have in your account

4. (a) Responses could include:
- Identify the vacancy (max 1)
- Carry out a job analysis, examine the vacancy to identify the tasks and skills of the position
- Create a job description, states the tasks and responsibilities of the job
  - Includes the conditions of the post, e.g. pay, hours
- Create a person specification, the skills and qualifications the ideal candidate would possess
  - Essential and desirable characteristics can be defined within this document
- Advertise the job – to enable the vacancy to be seen by applicants either internally or externally.
  - Internally on the organisation's intranet, noticeboard etc.
  - Externally in newspapers, job centres etc.
- Send out application forms (max 1)

(b) Responses could include:
- Pre-employment online screening to assess the suitability of applicants
  - Identical basic questions for anyone who wishes to apply
  - Helps narrow down the list to those most suited
- Online application forms
- Internet job websites
- Online tests and assessments
  - This may be the first stage of selection before an interview
- Database to record details of interviewees
  - To search for potential candidates with a specific skill or qualification
- Telephone interviews through conference calling
- Video conferencing through smartphones
- Word processing to create application forms

(c) Responses could include:
- Make the workplace safe and prevent risks to health
  - Ensure that plant and machinery is maintained and safe to use
  - Make sure that all materials are handled, stored and used safely
  - Provide adequate first aid facilities
  - Make sure that all facilities meet health and safety requirements, e.g. ventilation
  - Check that the correct work equipment is provided and is properly used and regularly maintained
  - Take precautions against the risks caused by flammable or explosive hazards, electrical equipment, noise and radiation
  - Avoid potentially dangerous work involving manual handling
  - Provide protective clothing or equipment free of charge
  - Ensure that the right warning signs are provided and looked after
  - Carry out risk assessments
- Create a Health and Safety policy
- Ensure Health and Safety training is conducted regularly
  - When new legislation is issued
  - Regular reminders, e.g. evacuation procedures

5. (a) Responses could include:
- Will avoid over-stocking and under-stocking
  - As stock levels will be known at all times
- Reduces the need for stock-taking
- Can be linked to supplier to order goods
- Can identify best sellers/non-movers
  - Which will help managers make decisions on promotions
- Up-to-date stock levels can be found instantly
  - Providing customers with accurate information
- Stock can be re-ordered automatically when the re-order level is reached
- Allows the organisation to keep track of stock rotation dates/perishable items
- Large amounts of information can be generated
  - That is useful for decision making purposes
  - Can search through large amounts of information quickly

(b) Responses could include any of the following:
- By reducing waste
  - This will help to reduce the amount of rubbish going to landfill sites
  - Using quality management processes
- By recycling packaging/waste products
  - To meet their environmental aims
- Solar panels/wind turbines could be used to help generate some of the electricity used in the production of products
  - This will reduce their energy bills
- They could have special controls fitted to lights so they automatically switch off
  - This will help to reduce expenses for the organisation
- Organic raw materials can be used

(c) (i) Responses could include:
- (Quality) raw materials
- Trained staff
- Good recruitment and selection process
- Maintained equipment
- Up-to-date equipment

(ii) Responses could include:
- Quality raw materials will result in a high quality finished product
- Improve customer satisfaction
  - Customers are likely to recommend products
- Helps to improve the image of the organisation
- Will reduce the number of accidents in the workplace
  - Can meet safety targets
- Fewer returns of faulty products
  - Reduces cost to the organisation

6. (a) (i) Responses could include:

Product
- To ensure the product/service meets the customer needs
- Packaging has to protect the product and make it appealing to the customer

Price
- What the customer has to pay for the product/service
- To set price to ensure the business covers its costs to make a profit
- If price too high customers may shop at competitors instead

Place
- Where the customer will purchase the good or service from
- Includes website, high street shop
- Distribution methods

(ii) Responses could include:
- BOGOF – buy one get one free
- Bonus packs – getting % extra for the same price
- Free gift within the packs
- Discounted prices for a limited period
- Free samples to encourage customers to try a product
- Loyalty cards – receive points for purchases
- Competitions to win prizes
- Celebrity endorsement whereby a celebrity is paid to use the product
  - Encourages fans of the celebrity to buy this to be like their hero

(b) Responses could include:

Costs
- The information may be out of date
  - This will mean the decision made on this may not be accurate
- All the information is available to all your competitors
  - The organisation does not have the competitive edge
- Information may be written from a bias point of view
  - As you are unsure of the reasons for gathering the information
- Information may not be relevant to the organisation's needs

Benefits
- Information already exists therefore quicker to obtain
- Large amounts of information available
- Relatively inexpensive to gather and obtain
  - Researchers do not need interview training
  - Time is not wasted standing in streets etc. trying to get first hand information

NATIONAL 5 BUSINESS MANAGEMENT 2016

Questions that ask candidates to **Describe** . . .
Candidates must make a number of relevant, factual points up to the total mark allocation for the question. These should be key points. The points do not need to be in any particular order. Candidates may provide a number of straightforward points or a smaller number of developed points, or a combination of these.

Up to the total mark allocation for this question:
- 1 mark should be given for each accurate relevant point of knowledge.
- a second mark could be given for any point that is developed from the point of knowledge.

Questions that ask candidates to **Explain** . . .
Candidates must make a number of points that relate cause and effect and/or make the relationships between things clear, for example by showing connections between a process/situation. These should be key reasons and may include theoretical concepts. There is no need to prioritise the reasons.

Candidates may provide a number of straightforward reasons or a smaller number of developed reasons, or a combination of these.

Up to the total mark allocation for this question:
- 1 mark should be given for each accurate relevant point of reason.
- a second mark could be given for any other point that is developed from the same reason.

Section 1

1. (a) (i) Sole trader

(ii) Responses could include:
- From the case study – Gemma likes to offer a personal and tailored service to her customers to meet their needs
- Providing extra assistance to a customer to ensure that their needs are completely satisfied

(b) Responses could include:

Costs
- Web hosting
- Website development and maintenance
- Postage charges for sending out goods to customers

Benefits
- Increased market share
- Ability to operate nationally/internationally
- "Free" advertising

(c) Responses could include:
- Advertising, e.g. radio, newspaper
- Customer demonstrations
- Free offers
- Competitions
- Discounts

(d) Responses could include:
- Staff get better at their job
- Increased motivation
- It is easier to introduce changes
- The image of the organisation is improved
- Staff become more flexible

(e) Responses could include:
- Rent
- Electricity
- Business rates
- Advertising

2. (a) (i) Responses could include:
- It reuses unwanted materials
- It reduces the amount of waste going to landfill
- Employ refugees
- Not using 'sweatshop' conditions

(ii) Responses could include:
- Limits the amount of waste going to landfill
- Improves the image of the organisation
- Increases sales/profits
- Can be used as a USP
  - Can give a competitive edge
  - Can win awards
- Can reduce costs if waste materials are used

(b) Responses could include:
- Access to more customers thus chances of increased market share/profit
- Access to customer information thereby allowing it to target products/marketing to those most likely to buy
- Can gain customer feedback thereby can change things to gain better customer satisfaction
- Customers can shop 24/7 which gives the organisation maximum time for customers to buy
- Can show entire product line thereby increasing customer choice
- Reduces costs as fixtures and fittings for shops are not required

(c) (i) Responses could include:
- On the job
- Induction training

(ii) Responses could include:

On the job
- Employees become familiar with surroundings
- May be cheaper than other forms of training
- Employees are actually productive
- Tailored to company needs

Induction
- Employees will feel at ease
- Employees will become familiar with the people and the surroundings
- Employees will become aware of health and safety issues

(d) Responses could include:

Application Form/CV
- These contain personal information on a candidate
- They can be used to compare against the person specification

Interview
- Allows the organisation to ask a series of questions
  - To allow for comparisons
- Allows the organisation to assess the candidate's appearance/personality
- Allows them to question the content of the CV/ application form
- Allows a candidate to ask questions

Reference
- Provides key information on attendance, attitude, time-keeping
- Usually written by a past employer

- Allows an organisation to confirm the content of a CV/application form

Testing
- These provide additional information on a candidate's suitability through practical assessment
- An organisation can see how a candidate copes under pressure

(e) Responses could include:

Quality Circles
- Small groups of employees who meet regularly to discuss how to improve methods of working

Quality Assurance
- Checking at every stage of the production process
  - To ensure 'right first time' and prevent errors

Quality Control
- Checking at the beginning and the end of production process only

Quality Standards
- When the product reaches the required standard it can be awarded a quality logo
  - Gives consumers confidence

Quality Inputs
- Raw materials need to be quality in order to obtain a quality final product
- All staff must be trained so they are competent and are all working to the same quality standards
- Machines need to be maintained so that they do not make mistakes affecting quality

Benchmarking
- Trying to match the standard of the quality leader/competitor

Section 2

3. (a) (i) Responses could include:
- Staff/HR
- Management/HR
- Finance
- Technology

(ii) Responses could include:

Staff
- If staff are trained they will be more productive
- If staff are more motivated they may produce a higher quality service
- If staff feel they have a say in decision making they may be more loyal to the organisation

Finance
- If there is a surplus of cash then the organisation may be able to make improvements
- If there is a lack of finance cost cutting measures need to be considered

Management
- If their objectives differ from the organisation's then the overall strategic aims of the business may not be met
- The quality of their decisions e.g. the range of goods they decide to stock can mean that the organisation improves customer satisfaction

Technology
- Having up-to-date technology will allow the organisation to produce quality products
- Having up-to-date technology may give the firm a competitive edge

(b) Responses could include:
- Provide a service to others
- Raise awareness of issues
- Better service for the community
- Creating a better reputation
- Ensuring finances are kept within budget
- Be socially responsible

(c) Responses could include:

Advantages
- The owner is hands-on to provide a personal service
- Owners get to keep all their profits
- Easy to set-up
  - Fewer legal restrictions
- Can make all the decisions
  - This is faster as no arguments

Disadvantages
- Limited access to finance
- No-one to consult or share ideas with
- Difficult to take time off for holidays or if off sick
- Liability is unlimited
  - The owners may lose their personal possessions in order to meet the debts of the organisation

4. (a) (i) Responses could include:

Word processing package
- Create a job advert/application form
- Key in a job or person specification
- Letter to applicants about interview/successful appointments/unsuccessful notification

(ii) **Database package**
- Record of applicants
- Record of posts available

(iii) **Company website**
- Online application form
- Electronic job and person specifications could be accessed online
- Contact us feature to apply for jobs
- Internal jobs could be posted on the website

(b) (i) Responses could include:
- Sit in
- Overtime ban
- Work to rule
- Go slow
- Strike
- Boycott
- Lock out
- Protest/picket line

(ii) Responses could include:
- Production within the organisation may come to a halt therefore the organisation could struggle to produce goods to meet customer demand
  - Causing customers to go elsewhere
- Decreased levels of production could damage the reputation of the organisation
- An organisation could lose customers as goods not produced within an acceptable timescale
- Employees refusing to work overtime or going slow would mean deadlines not met
  - Creating a poor image or reputation
- Company's share price may fall due to the poor reputation of the firm

(c) Responses could include:
- Software packages with remote access allow flexible working arrangements

- Video conferencing allows meetings employees between different locations
  - Less travel time and cost are incurred
- Email allows an employee to communicate with their job share partner/communicate with the office from home
  - Easier access to others with the use of email
- Allows work to be completed outside of 'traditional' working hours
- Less office space required as staff may be working from home using laptops
- Electronic documents can be shared and stored on the cloud/intranet to be used out with the office

5. (a) (i) Responses could include:
- Increasing wages
- Increasing purchases
- £20,000 spent on capital expenditure
- Negative closing balance in May and June

(ii) Responses could include:
- Do not allow overtime
- Reduce the number of workers to reduce wages
- Find a cheaper supplier to reduce cost of purchases
  - Negotiate discounts for bulk buying or prompt payment
- Purchasing the van on hire purchase
  - To spread payments
- Lease or rent the van rather than buying it outright
- Arrange for an overdraft to cover negative closing balance.
- Take out a bank loan to boost receipts

(b) (i) Responses could include:
- Advertising

(ii) Responses could include:
- Purchases
- Wages

(c) Responses could include:
- To calculate gross profit
- To calculate the cost of sales
- To show net sales
- To calculate the total cost of expenses
- To calculate profit for the year/net profit
- To show other incomes
- For legal reasons
- To aid decision making
- For tax reasons

6. (a) Responses could include:

Job
- Where a one off/unique product is made
- Each job is started and finished before moving on to the next

Batch
- When groups of similar products are produced
- Machinery is stopped, cleaned etc. before being used for a different batch

Flow
- A continuous process is used and goods move along a production line from beginning to end
- Large volumes can be made in a short period of time
- Each product is identical

(b) Responses could include:
- Price reflects the quality given
- Quality of the raw materials is consistent
- Delivery time meets the needs of the organisation
- The supplier can deliver the correct quantity
- The level of credit being offered by the supplier
- The length of credit period being offered by the supplier
- Location of supplier as it will impact on delivery charges/time

(c) Responses could include:

Under stocking
- Becomes harder to cope with unexpected changes in demand which means customers may go elsewhere to purchase the product
  - If customers go elsewhere they may lose them completely and not just the one time
- Production may have to stop completely meaning paying for workers who aren't producing any goods
- Continually ordering or restocking can mean increased administration costs
  - Increased transport costs
- Increased unit costs due to not bulk buying

Over stocking
- Carry large amounts of stock will increase the cost of storage which reduces profit
  - May result in having to pay larger insurance costs
  - Increased security costs
- Capital is tied up in stock which means that the money cannot be used elsewhere
- The stock may deteriorate resulting in larger wastage costs
- Changes in trends and fashion will mean that stock might become obsolete and not be able to be sold
- Higher risk of theft as it is less obvious when stock has gone missing

NATIONAL 5 BUSINESS MANAGEMENT 2017

Questions that ask candidates to **Describe** ...
Candidates must make a number of relevant, factual points up to the total mark allocation for the question. These should be key points. The points do not need to be in any particular order. Candidates may provide a number of straightforward points or a smaller number of developed points, or a combination of these.

Up to the total mark allocation for this question:
- 1 mark should be given for each accurate relevant point of knowledge
- a second mark could be given for any point that is developed from the point of knowledge

Questions that ask candidates to **Explain** ...
Candidates must make a number of points that relate cause and effect and/or make the relationships between things clear, for example by showing connections between a process/situation. These should be key reasons and may include theoretical concepts. There is no need to prioritise the reasons.

Candidates may provide a number of straightforward reasons or a smaller number of developed reasons, or a combination of these.

Up to the total mark allocation for this question:
- 1 mark should be given for each accurate relevant point of reason
- a second mark could be given for any other point that is developed from the same reason

Questions that ask candidates to **Compare** ...
Candidates must demonstrate a true comparison (like with like) in order to gain any mark. Both sides of the point must be clear but need not be linked (can be matched up). Candidates can write several points regarding the first comparison item followed by several points on the second and the marker match the points using codes (e.g. a, b, c).

Up to the total mark allocation for this question:
- 1 mark should be given for each compared point

Section 1

1. (a) (i) Responses should include:
- Restaurant reviews in newspapers
- Branding
- Shop/Shop Premises
- Website
- Social Media (accept names – e.g. Facebook, Twitter, etc.)

(ii) Responses could include:
- Brand advertises/promotes the product which increases brand recognition
  - Reduces spending on promotion/increases sales/increases profits
- Customer loyalty which will lead to repeat purchases
- Perception of quality which means customers will choose over rivals
- Ability to charge higher prices which leads to increased revenues/profits

(b) (i) Responses could include:
- Road
- Sea
- Rail
- Air

(ii) Responses could include:

Road
- Direct distribution
- Cheaper than rail/air transport
- Difficult to carry large amounts
- Slower method of distribution compared with sea/rail/air
- Not environmentally friendly
  - Increases pollution

Sea
- Cheaper than rail/air transport
- Large items can be transported
- Slower method of transport than road/rail/air
- Requires additional transport/not direct

Rail
- Large items can be transported
- Quicker than road/sea
- Reduces carbon footprint
- Requires additional transport/not direct

Air
- Fast method of distribution
- Expensive method

(c) Responses could include:

Political
- Health and safety standards affect the business as they will have to train staff to follow guidelines
  - Will increase costs to provide these
- Health and safety standards affect the business as they will have to provide safety equipment/clothing
- EU legislation protects the brand name
  - Reduces impact of competitors

Competition
- Rivals could try to steal customers from the business
  - Which would reduce sales/profits/market share

Technology
- Social media increases customer awareness

Social
- Change in taste can lead to increased/higher demand

(d) Responses could include:
- A sole trader is owned by one person whereas a private limited company is owned by shareholders
- A sole trader is run by an individual whereas a private limited company is run by a managing director/board of directors
- A sole trader makes the decisions in a business whereas a managing director/board of directors/shareholders make decisions in a private limited company
- Sole traders have unlimited liability whereas private limited companies have limited liability
- Both belong to the private sector of the economy
- Legal documents required on forming a private limited company whereas a sole trader does not require any formal paperwork

2. (a) (i) Responses should include:
- Lifestyle
- Health conscious
- Beauty conscious
- Chocolate lovers
- Ethical buyers
- Organic buyers

(ii) Responses could include:
- Able to adapt product to suit target market
- Pricing strategy will be appropriate to target market
- Appropriate places to sell product will be chosen
- Reduces likelihood of wasted investment in wrong product/promotions
- Can offer a range of products to suit different markets

(b) (i) Responses could include:
- Batch production – where a group of identical products are made with all processes being carried out simultaneously
- Flow production – where products are made in stages on a production line with processes being added at each stage

(ii) Responses could include:

Batch

Advantages
- Large amounts can be made
- Batches can be customised
  - Meeting customer needs
- Economies of scale gained

Disadvantages
- Expensive initial outlay for equipment
- Careful production planning required
- Equipment needs to be cleaned between batches
- Mistakes may lead to loss of whole batch
  - This can lead to a loss of profits

Flow

Advantages
- High quantity of products
- Standardisation of quality of products
- Economies of scale gained
  - Lower cost per unit of production
- Machines can work 24/7

Disadvantages
- Expensive initial outlay for equipment
- Maintenance costs
- Lack of output if machines are broken

(c) Responses could include:
- More expensive to purchase environmentally friendly/hybrid vehicles, e.g. LPG fuel/electric
- Reduces environmental damage/pollution
- Costs of using ethical suppliers may be higher
- Helps business to meet government targets
- Efficiency may fall, ethical distribution may reduce amount of deliveries
- Gives a competitive edge over rivals
- Creates a positive image for the business/good CSR
  - Customer loyalty could increase

(d) Responses should include:

Owners
- Make decisions this could affect product development
- Invest more money which can aid expansion

Suppliers
- Can increase price which increased production cost
  - This reduces profit margins

Customers/Independent Retailers/Health Centres
- Customer satisfaction will impact upon sales and revenues
- Customer loyalty which means repeat purchases
- Customer recommendations which leads to increased sales

Section 2

3. (a) (i) Responses could include:
- Private
- Public
- Third/voluntary

(ii) Responses could include:
- Both the third and public sector organisations have the objective to make a difference
- Private sector organisations have an objective to make a profit whereas a public sector organisation has the objective to use public funds effectively
- Third sector organisations have an objective to increase awareness/sales whereas public sector organisation has the objective to provide a service
- All sectors have the objective to be socially responsible

(b) Responses could include:
- Have a good aftersales service
- Have a returns policy
- Ensure all staff are highly trained
- Keep staff motivated
- Use quality indicators to measure performance
- Recruit suitable staff, e.g. helpful, polite, etc.
- Use high quality raw materials/quality control
- Ensure system of customer feedback is in place

(c) Responses could include:
- A lack of finance means not having enough money to carry out expansion plans
- Having excess finances that enables an organisation to train staff, invest in more equipment etc.
- If staff are skilled they will provide good quality customer service
- The morale of staff to carry out their jobs to a high standard
- Available technology used within the organisation could increase the rate of production
- If technology breaks down this can result in delays in production
- If managers are inexperienced they could make poor decisions

4. (a) Responses could include:

Job description
- States the tasks and responsibilities of the job
  - Includes the conditions of the post, e.g. pay, hours

Person specification
- Describes the ideal candidate for the post
  - Contains the essential and desirable characteristics
  - Skills, qualities and qualifications necessary to do the job

Job advert
- Usually contains aspects of the job description and person specification
  - Could be placed internally or externally
  - Internally on the organisation's intranet, noticeboards etc.
  - Externally in newspapers, job centres etc.

Application form
- Standard form sent out by an organisation for candidates to complete using personal details

(b) Responses could include:
- Internal recruitment ensures candidates already have knowledge of the organisation, however external recruitment can attract candidates with new ideas

- Internal recruitment is fast as candidates are already in the organisation, however external recruitment can take a very long time
- Internal recruitment is more cost effective as advertising can be done on staff newsletters or intranet, whereas external recruitment can be very expensive in costs of advertising
- Internal recruitment can create another vacancy, whereas external recruitment adds a new employee to the staff
- Internal recruitment is motivating for staff who see a promotion path, however external recruitment may cause conflict with existing staff
- Internal vacancies can be advertised on noticeboards and via email, whereas external vacancies can be advertised using websites and job centres

(c) Responses could include:
- Employees who are trained will have better skills meaning a higher quality output
- Employees who are trained will be more efficient at their job which means productivity will increase
- Employees will be more motivated which means they are less likely to be absent
- Employees may gain qualifications which may give them more incentive to remain with the organisations
- Employees may be able to gain experience which can help them to achieve promotion

(d) Responses could include:
- Protection against discrimination
- Protected characteristics
- Age/sex/sexual orientation/gender re-assignment/disability/race, religion or belief/marriage or civil partnership/pregnancy and maternity
- Includes workplace victimisation, harassment and bullying

5. (a) Responses could include:

Internet
- Ordering inventory online

Database/EPOS
- The use of bar codes can be used to keep a running total of inventory in hand
- It can be useful for the re-ordering of inventory as can be linked directly to supplier
- It can help staff to locate inventory within the warehouse

CAM (Computer Aided Manufacture)
- Could be used to help control the machinery of the business
- This would allow for capital intensive production to run smoothly

CAD (Computer Aided Design)
- Could be used to help design products on a computer screen
- This would allow for problems to be solved before prototypes are made

GPS
- Could allow an organisation to keep track of deliveries

(b) (i) Responses could include:

Quality control
- Quality is checked at the beginning (inputs) and end (outputs) of the production process only
- Unacceptable products are either scrapped or put back for reworking

Quality assurance
- Quality is checked at every stage of the production process
- Mistakes are found early in the process
  - Less waste

Quality inputs
- Ensuring that raw materials are the best that they can be to ensure a quality output
- Ensuring that machinery and equipment is up-to-date and fully serviced so that it is working to its best at all times
- Ensuring the recruitment process gets the best staff
- Training staff to ensure they can produce goods to the best quality

(ii) Responses could include:

Maximum inventory (stock) level
- The highest level of inventory that should be held at any one time

Lead time
- The time from placing the order to the goods being delivered

6. (a) Responses should include:
- A – Sales revenue/Sales/Revenue
- B – 30,000
- C – 20,000

(b) (i) Responses could include:
- Retained profits – reinvested from previous years
- Share issue – selling shares to friends and family (Ltd)
- Bank loan – money borrowed from the bank repaid with interest/OR in instalments
- Government grant – money received from the government that does not need to be repaid
- Overdraft – taking more money out of your bank account than is present in your account
- Mortgage – money borrowed to buy property
- Hire purchase – purchasing assets and repaying over time with interest
- Leasing – renting equipment/assets

(ii) Responses could include:

Retained profits
- Cash is readily available
- Does not have to be paid back
- No interest charged

Share issue
- No interest charged
- Does not have to be repaid

Bank loan
- Repaid in instalments
  - Aids budgeting

Government grant
- Does not need to be paid back

Overdraft
- Easy to arrange
- Only pay interest on amount borrowed

Mortgage
- Repaid over a long period of time
- Large amount can be raised

Hire purchase
- Costs spread over a period of time
- Helps cash flow issues

Leasing
- Can acquire an expensive asset without a capital outlay
- Easier to change equipment when it becomes obsolete

(c) Responses could include:
- To make comparisons between actual and projected figures
- Take corrective action
- To allow the organisation to make better decisions
- Identify surplus of cash/identify a deficit
- To set targets
- Budgets can be used to plan for the future

NATIONAL 5 BUSINESS MANAGEMENT 2017 SPECIMEN QUESTION PAPER

Questions that ask candidates to **Describe** . . .
Candidates must make a number of relevant, factual points up to the total mark allocation for the question. These should be key points. The points do not need to be in any particular order. Candidates may provide a number of straightforward points or a smaller number of developed points, or a combination of these.

Up to the total mark allocation for this question:
- 1 mark should be given for each accurate relevant point of knowledge
- a second mark could be given for any point that is developed from the point of knowledge.

Questions that ask candidates to **Explain** . . .
Candidates must make a number of points that relate cause and effect and/or make the relationships between things clear, for example by showing connections between a process/situation. These should be key reasons and may include theoretical concepts. There is no need to prioritise the reasons. Candidates may provide a number of straightforward reasons or a smaller number of developed reasons, or a combination of these.

Up to the total mark allocation for this question:
- 1 mark should be given for each accurate relevant point of reason
- a second mark could be given for any other point that is developed from the same reason.

Questions that ask candidates to **Compare** . . .
Candidates must demonstrate a true comparison in order to gain any mark. Both sides of the point must be clear but need not be linked. Candidates can write several points regarding the first comparison item, followed by several points on the second, and the marker match the points using codes (e.g. a, b, c).

Up to the total mark allocation for this question:
- 1 mark should be given for each compared point

1. (a) (i) Responses could include:
- They do not add any artificial colourings etc.
- They recycle their waste by turning it into feed for pigs
- Using labour rather than machines (hand pressed)

(ii) Responses could include:
- Limits the amount of waste going to landfill
- Helps to win awards
- Reduce costs/increase costs
- Can charge a higher price
- Improves the image of the organisation
  - This could increase sales/profits
- Can be used as a USP
  - Can give a competitive edge

(b) Responses could include:
- Job Production
  - More labour intensive
  - One product is made at a time
  - Uses skilled labour
  - Production costs are higher
  - Can customise individual products
  - More motivating as the product changes

Whereas
- Flow Production
  - More capital intensive
  - Multiple products are made at a time
  - Uses unskilled labour

  - Can spread cost over multiple units/can benefit from economies of scale
  - Creates standardised products
  - Less motivating as task is repetitive
- Both methods of production can be expensive in terms of staff training and machinery

(c) (i) Responses could include:
- More profitable to produce than cider
- 67% of customers rated "all natural" as the most interesting products
- 60% globally say they are interested in products with proven health benefits

(ii) Responses could include:

Political
- Changes in laws may prevent Cuddybridge from operating, which will result in it having to spend extra finance to comply with the changes
- Local council may refuse to give planning permission, which means that the company cannot grow

Economic
- There may be a reduction in consumer spending due to recession, which will reduce sales
- Cost of producing the apple juice may rise due to inflation, which will increase variable costs

Social
- There may be an increase in publicity about healthy drinks, which may increase sales

Technological
- A new piece of equipment may become available, which would increase the speed of the pressing

Environmental
- Weather may be bad, which could result in a shortage of apples
  - This could halt production
- There may be increased consumer awareness of environmental issues, which may mean Cuddybridge may have to adapt packaging

(d) Responses could include:

Quality Circles
- Small groups of employees who meet regularly to discuss how to improve methods of working

Quality Assurance
- Checking at every stage of the production process
- To ensure 'right first time' and prevent errors

Quality Control
- Checking at (the beginning and) the end of production process only

Quality Inputs
- Raw materials need to be high quality in order to obtain a quality final product
- All staff must be trained so they are competent and are all working to the same quality standards
- Machines need to be maintained so that they do not make mistakes affecting quality

(e) (i) Road

(ii) Responses could include:
- Juice is delivered directly to the customer (door to door)
- Juice can be transported in refrigerated vans
- Cuddybridge can deliver at any time of the day or night
- Clients are local so air (or sea) is not suitable

2\. (a) (i) Responses could include:
- On the Job
- Off the Job

(ii) Responses could include:

On the Job

Advantages
- Employees become familiar with surroundings
- May be cheaper than other forms of training
  - As existing staff can train others
- Employees are productive during training
- Training is specific to the organisation
- Takes place in work time so employees may be happier to take part

Disadvantages
- Takes a current employee away from production
  - Reduces the amount produced
- Employees may make mistakes whilst learning
  - Results in increased wastage/lower customer satisfaction

Off the Job

Advantages
- Employees may gain a qualification
  - This could result in them being considered for promotion
- Wider range of skills can be gained
  - Improves staff flexibility
- Can learn from outside experts

Disadvantages
- No production takes place
- Expensive as have to pay for the course/outside training providers
  - Also pay for staff travel expenses
- May need to hire a supply/temporary worker

(b) Responses could include:

Application Form/CV
- A document which contains personal information on a candidate
  - They can be used to compare against the person specification
  - Can be used to decide who is short-listed for interview/who is rejected

Interview
- A face to face meeting where an applicant is asked questions
  - Allows the organisation to ask a series of questions to all applicants to allow for comparisons
  - Allows the organisation to assess the candidate's appearance/personality
  - Allows the organisation to question the content of the CV/application form
  - Allows a candidate to ask questions

Reference
- A written or oral report on the work ethic of an applicant provided by a previous employer
  - Provides key information on attendance, attitude, time-keeping
  - Usually written by a past employer
  - Allows an organisation to confirm the content of a CV/application form

Testing
- A physical or mental challenge for the applicant
  - These provide additional information on a candidate's suitability

- An organisation can see how a candidate copes under pressure

(c) Responses could include:
- Fifteen aims to help young people whereas a private sector organisation aims to grow
- Both Fifteen and a private sector organisation aim to make a profit
- Both Fifteen and a private sector organisation aim to provide a service

(d) Responses could include:
- Consumers are attracted to the product, in an attempt to be like the celebrity
- Jamie Oliver is already a household name, so Fifteen could save money on marketing
- Higher prices can be charged, which will result in greater profits
- Greater chance of success, as Jamie Oliver will already have brand loyalty

(e) Responses could include:

Marketing
- Internet could be used to allow customers to book tables online
- Internet could be used to gather customer information through online surveys
- MS Publisher could be used to create business cards/posters
- Apps could be created to inform customers
  - Send push notifications to increase awareness of products
  - Allow customers to purchase goods on the go
- Social media could be used to increase awareness of products/notify customers of special offers
  - These can be shared or re-tweeted to increase brand awareness
- QR codes could be used to create a link to Fifteen's website

Operations
- Ovens could be programmed to come on and go off at certain times of the day
- iPads could be used to take orders from customers
  - These would automatically send orders to the kitchen
- Databases could be used to create/maintain stock records/customer records
- Internet could be used to compare the prices of suppliers

(f) Responses could include:
- Find a cheaper supplier of ingredients
- Negotiate a cheaper rental agreement on restaurants
- Switch utility suppliers
- Reduce the amount of expenditure on advertising

3. (a) (i) Responses could include:
- Employees
- Shareholders/owners
- Government
- Suppliers
- Bank
- Local Community
- Customers

(ii) Responses could include:
- Employees
  - Could go on strike, preventing production
  - Could provide poor customer service, which will reduce sales
- Shareholders/owners
  - Could invest additional capital, allowing more efficient equipment to be purchased
    - This could reduce wastage
- Government
  - Could increase National Living Wage, which will increase wages
  - Could change taxation levels, resulting in lower profits
- Suppliers
  - Could deliver goods late, which would prevent production
    - This would result in disappointed customers
  - May increase prices, which will result in reduction of gross profit
- Bank
  - Could refuse an overdraft, making it more difficult to pay bills
- Local Community
  - Could protest about the business, leading to a bad reputation

(b) Responses could include:
- Train staff
  - So they are knowledgeable and can answer customer queries
- Maintain a clean environment
- Employ extra staff to cover busy periods
  - This will reduce queues
- Use effective pricing strategies
- Provide a quick response to complaints
- Provide a good aftersales service

(c) Responses could include:
- Sole Trader is owned by one person whereas an LTD owned by shareholders
- Sole Trader has unlimited liability whereas an LTD has limited liability
- Does not require any formal paperwork to begin trading whereas an LTD must prepare formal documents to be sent to Register House
- Sole Trader keeps all profits whereas an LTD splits profits (dividends) with the shareholders

4. (a) (i) Responses could include:
- The price the customers are willing to pay for it
- The price competitors are charging
- The stage of the product life cycle
- The image of the product
- The cost of the raw materials
- Location of retail outlet

(ii) Responses could include:
- Premium/High Price, where the price is set higher than competitor
- Market price, where prices are set at a similar level to competitors
- Low price, where prices are set lower than competitors

(b) Responses could include:
- Brand loyalty, which means you are guaranteed returning customers
- Brand recognition, so less advertising required
- Gives an illusion/image of quality, which means higher prices can be charged
- Easier to launch new products, due to customers being familiar with the brand

(c) Responses could include:
- Use technology to reduce the amount of paper used
- Ensure that adverts comply with discrimination laws, e.g. do not exploit women in adverts
- Ensure that adverts do not give misleading information
- Ensure that adverts do not offend customers' beliefs
- Ensure that there are no hidden costs in adverts

5. (a) Responses could include:
- Identify the vacancy
- Carry out a job analysis
- Create a job description
- Create a person specification
- Advertise the job
- Send out application forms

(b) Responses could include:
- Piece rate – employee is paid for each item they produce
- Time rate – employee paid for each hour they work
- Overtime – employee paid for working more than their contracted hours
  - This could be paid at a higher rate, e.g. time and a half, double time
- Bonus – an additional payment over and above normal salary
- Commission – employee is paid a percentage of their overall sales
- Salary – an annual amount paid in 12 equal instalments

(c) Responses could include:
- Equality Act
- Health and Safety at Work Act
- National Minimum Wage/National Living Wage Regulations
- Employment Rights Act

6. (a) (i) £20,000
(ii) £8,000

(b) Responses could include:

Bank loan
- Finance borrowed from a bank and repaid with interest
  - Paid back in instalments
  - Paid over a long period of time
  - Interest is payable on amount borrowed

Grant
- Cash given to a business by the government
  - Cash does not need to be repaid
  - Complex paperwork will need to be completed
  - Set criteria may need to be met

Overdraft
- Can take more cash out than you have in your account
  - Suitable for short-term cash flow problems
  - Cash available quickly as it can be prearranged

Share Issue
- People are invited to buy a part ownership of a business
  - Investment does not need to be repaid
  - Large amounts can be raised
  - Control is not lost to outsiders
  - Dividends will need to be paid

(c) Responses could include:
- Formulae can be used to calculate information
  - Which allows for automatic calculation if anything changes
  - Which reduces error
- Information can be saved and edited later
- Templates can be used for financial information, e.g. Cash Budgets/Profit Statements
- Standardisation of documents means that processes are easily replicated
- Graphs/Charts can be created to display information
  - Which allows easier comparison of complex financial information

(d) Responses could include:
- To calculate gross profit
- To calculate the cost of sales
- To show net sales
- To calculate the total cost of expenses
- To calculate profit for the year/net profit
- To show other incomes
- For legal reasons
- To aid decision making
- For tax reasons

7. (a) Responses could include:
- Is the price reasonable?
- Is the quality acceptable?
- Quality of the raw materials is consistent
- Delivery time meets the needs of the organisation
- The supplier can deliver the correct quantity
- The length of credit period being offered by the supplier
- Location of supplier as it will impact on delivery charges/time
- Discounts that could be given for bulk buying
- Is the supplier reliable/do they deliver on time?

(b)

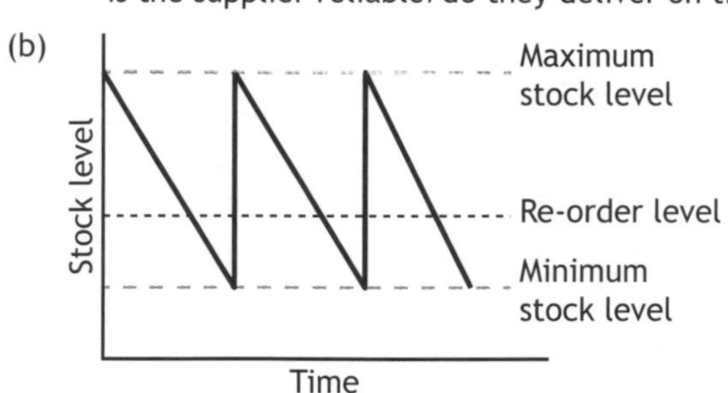

(c) Responses could include:

Overstocking
- Carrying large amounts of stock will increase the cost of storage, which reduces profit
  - May result in having to pay larger insurance costs
  - Increased security costs
- Capital is tied up in stock, which means that the finance cannot be used elsewhere
- The stock may deteriorate, resulting in larger wastage costs
- Changes in trends and fashion will mean that stock might become obsolete, which means it will not be able to be sold
- Higher risk of theft, as it is less obvious that stock has gone missing

Understocking
- Becomes harder to cope with unexpected changes in demand, which means customers may go elsewhere to purchase the product
  - If customers go elsewhere the firm may lose them completely and not just the one time
- Production may have to stop completely, meaning paying for workers who are not producing any goods
- Need to continually order or restock, which can mean increased administration costs
  - Increased transport costs
- No bulk buying, therefore increased unit costs

Acknowledgements

Permission has been sought from all relevant copyright holders and Hodder Gibson is grateful for the use of the following:

Logo © The Factory Skatepark (2015 page 2);
Logo © Trespass (2015 page 4);
Logo © Commonwealth Games Federation (2015 page 4);
An extract and logo from www.justdogsshop.co.uk © Just Dogs (2016 page 2);
Logo © Who Made Your Pants/Becky John (2016 page 3);
An article and photo about Charles Macleod Stornoway Black Pudding. Reproduced by permission of Charles Macleod Ltd (2017 page 2);
Image © margo555/stock.adobe.com (2017 page 3);
Information and logo taken from www.iqchoc.com. Reproduced by kind permission of iQ Superfood Chocolate (2017 page 3);
Information and logo reproduced by kind permission of Cuddybridge Apple Juice (www.cuddybridgeapplejuice.com) (SQP page 2);
Infographic from 'Tetra Pak® 2016 Juice Index Report' and statistics from Mintel GNPD 2015 (Vegetable Nutrition), Tetra Pak consumer survey (All Natural) and Roper Reports Worldwide 2015 (Speciality 100% Juice). Reproduced by permission of Tetra Pak (SQP page 2);
Infographic from 'Changing Tastes: The UK Soft Drinks Annual Report 2015' © The British Soft Drinks Association and statistics from Zenith International (SQP page 2);
A passage adapted from www.fifteen.net © Jamie Oliver Food Foundation (SQP page 4);
Image © Yui Mok/PA Archive/PA Images (SQP page 4);
A logo and extract from 'Channel4Dispatches – Supermarkets: Brexit & Your Shrinking Shop' © Channel 4 TV (SQP page 4).